Disappearing Ice

Written by Kerrie Shanahan

Series Consultant: Linda Hoyt

WorldWise
Content-based Learning

Contents

Introduction

A polar bear stands on a large sheet of ice in the **Arctic**. She is hunting. Her sense of smell tells her that seals are not far away. The seals are hunting, too. They feed on Arctic cod, which swim underneath the massive sheets of ice that cover the ocean.

Sadly, this polar bear is struggling to find enough food – her icy home is in trouble. The ice is melting, causing many problems for this polar bear, and for most animals of the Arctic.

Chapter 1
The Arctic: An icy home

The **Arctic** is the most northern part of the earth. It is a cold, harsh place, made up of land and water.

The water in the ocean is so cold that it freezes, and some of the ocean stays covered in large sheets of ice all year round.

The land in the Arctic is covered in ice and snow most of the year. No trees grow here because it is too cold.

But the animals that live in the Arctic are able to survive in this frozen world. They have ways of getting the food they need, and to stay safe from **predators**.

Arctic Circle

Animals of the Arctic

Polar bear

Seal

Arctic fox

Narwhal

Arctic cod

Ice in the Arctic

The ice floating on top of the ocean is called **pack ice**.
Pack ice is not connected to land or the ocean floor. It
is moved around by the wind and **water currents**.

The amount of pack ice changes as the weather changes. In summer, the pack ice sheets break up into smaller pieces, which slowly melt away.

Icy fact

Most sheets of pack ice are between 30 and 180 centimetres thick, but some can be up to six metres thick.

Chapter 2
A changing habitat

The earth is becoming warmer, the **climate** is changing, and the **Arctic** is changing, too.

Shrinking pack ice

The amount of **pack ice** in the Arctic is shrinking.

Because the Arctic is warmer than it used to be, more pack ice is melting earlier each summer. Winters are not as cold as they used to be, and there is less pack ice.

What happens to Arctic animals when there is less pack ice?

Did you know?

Some scientists estimate that in just over 20 years there might be no ice in the Arctic during summer.

Orcas

Narwhals

Chapter 3
Impact on animals

Arctic animals need **pack ice**. Some use it to stay safe from **predators**, some move around on the ice to find a mate, and some use it to hunt for food.

Having less ice is affecting Arctic animals. Some are in danger of becoming **extinct**.

Staying safe

Some animals use pack ice to keep safe from predators.

Narwhals swim into cracks between the **ice sheets** to hide from orcas. But because there is now less pack ice, narwhals have fewer places to hide. They are more likely to be eaten by orcas or whales.

How big are narwhals?

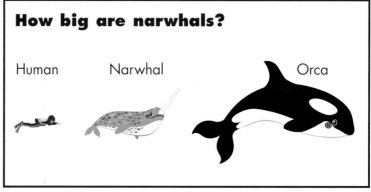

Human   Narwhal   Orca

The female ringed **seal** makes a den in the ice before she gives birth to her pup. The pup then stays in the icy den where it is safe. Now that the ice melts earlier, the pup has less time in its safe den.

Did you know?

Ringed seals have claws on their flippers that they use to dig holes in the ice. Snow forms a cover over the hole to make a safe, icy den.

Ringed seal

Moving around

Pack ice creates a huge area that animals can move around on. But once the ice melts, the animals can no longer do this.

Arctic foxes use the pack ice like a bridge to get from place to place. Now that the ice is melting faster and earlier, foxes sometimes get cut off from other foxes. This makes it more difficult to find a mate, and so fewer pups are born.

Hunting for food

Polar bears use the pack ice to hunt for seals to eat. They wait on top of the ice as the seals swim underneath. When a seal comes to the surface to breathe, the waiting polar bear catches it.

But because the ice is melting earlier, polar bears have less time to hunt for food.

Did you know?
Polar bears eat seals because seals are high in fat. The food the polar bears eat on land, when the ice has melted, is not high in fat.

Zooplankton

Food problems

Arctic animals have difficulty finding food when there is less pack ice. The food chain is affected.

Algae are tiny living things that grow on the bottom of pack ice. Algae are eaten by other tiny living things called **zooplankton**. But there is a problem.

There is not as much algae growing now because there is less pack ice for it to grow on.

So the zooplankton have fewer algae to feed on.

This means there are fewer zooplankton drifting in the water. Arctic cod feed on zooplankton, but now there is less food, and the cod may not grow and breed.

With fewer Arctic cod in the ocean, the seals do not have as much food, so their numbers are dropping.

And without seals, the polar bears do not have enough high-fat food. Without this high-fat food, they become too thin and cannot have cubs.

Arctic food chain

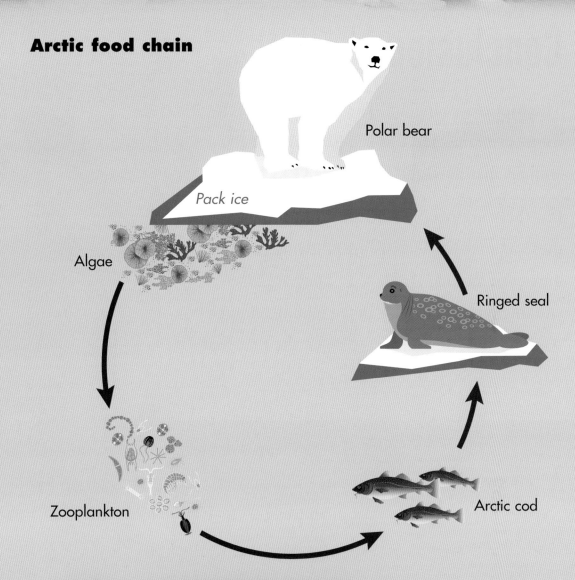

Polar bear

Pack ice

Algae

Ringed seal

Zooplankton

Arctic cod

Polar bear facts

- There are about 20,000–25,000 polar bears in the wild.

- Polar bears are listed as in danger. This means they are likely to become extinct if things don't improve for them.

Conclusion

The **Arctic** is changing. The amount of **pack ice** is shrinking, and this is a problem for the animals that need the ice to survive.

But there are people who are working to help these animals. Scientists are studying the impact of melting Arctic ice. They are also working on ways to slow down **climate change**. And this will hopefully slow down the rate that Arctic pack ice is disappearing.

Glossary

algae tiny living things that are neither plants nor animals; mostly found in water

Arctic the icy-cold area of the world that surrounds the North Pole

climate what the weather conditions are usually like, year after year, in a particular place

climate change when the usual patterns of the weather change

extinct when a group of living things no longer has any living members on Earth

ice sheets large, thick areas of ice

pack ice ice that floats on top of ocean water and is not connected to land or to the ocean floor

predators animals that get food by killing and eating other animals

water currents the natural movements of water that usually follow a certain pattern

zooplankton tiny, floating animals that live in water

Index